FISH PALS

PAT JACOBS

Crabtree Publishing Company

www.crabtreebooks.com

Crabtree Publishing Company
www.crabtreebooks.com
1-800-387-7650

Published in Canada
Crabtree Publishing
616 Welland Avenue
St. Catharines, ON
L2M 5V6

Published in the United States
Crabtree Publishing
PMB 59051
350 Fifth Ave, 59th Floor
New York, NY 10118

Published in 2019 by CRABTREE PUBLISHING COMPANY.

First published in 2019 by Wayland
Copyright © Hodder and Stoughton, 2019

Author: Pat Jacobs

Editors: Victoria Brooke, Petrice Custance

Project coordinator: Kathy Middleton

Cover and interior design: Dynamo

Proofreader: Melissa Boyce

Prepress technician: Samara Parent

Print and production coordinator: Katherine Berti

Photographs:
Shutterstock: p. 7 (top right), 23 (center left), 31 (bottom left)
All other images courtesy of Getty Images iStock

Printed in the U.S.A./012019/CG20181123

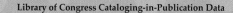

Library and Archives Canada Cataloguing in Publication

Jacobs, Pat, author
    Fish pals / Pat Jacobs.

(Pet pals)
Includes index.
Issued in print and electronic formats.
ISBN 978-0-7787-5501-2 (hardcover).--
ISBN 978-0-7787-5732-0 (softcover).--
ISBN 978-1-4271-2229-2 (HTML)

    1. Aquarium fishes--Juvenile literature. 2. Aquarium fishes--Behavior--Juvenile literature. I. Title.

SF457.25.J33 2018   j639.34   C2018-905536-7
                                    C2018-905537-5

Library of Congress Cataloging-in-Publication Data

Names: Jacobs, Pat, author.
Title: Fish pals / Pat Jacobs.
Description: New York, New York : Crabtree Publishing, 2019. |
  Series: Pet pals | Includes index.
Identifiers: LCCN 2018049840 (print) | LCCN 2018050491 (ebook)
  ISBN 9781427122292 (Electronic) |
  ISBN 9780778755012 (hardcover : alk. paper) |
  ISBN 9780778757320 (paperback : alk. paper)
Subjects: LCSH: Aquarium fishes--Juvenile literature. |
  Pets--Juvenile literature.
Classification: LCC SF457.25 (ebook) |
  LCC SF457.25 .J33 2019 (print) | DDC 639.34--dc23
LC record available at https://lccn.loc.gov/2018049840

CONTENTS

YOUR FISH
FROM HEAD TO TAIL

Fish were the first **vertebrates** on the planet. They have been swimming in our oceans, lakes, and rivers for more than 500 million years. Scientists believe there are more than 30,000 different **species** of fish alive today.

Dorsal fin: This stops a fish from rolling over in the water.

Caudal fins: These are also known as tail fins, and help to move the fish forward.

Anal fin: This keeps a fish **stable** as it swims.

Pelvic fins: These are found on each side of the fish. They help the fish turn and move up and down.

Lateral line: The lateral line is a row of sensors along a fish's side that detect the position of objects or vibrations from **predators** and **prey**.

Brain: Fish have good memories and can remember routes, people, and signals that it is feeding time, sometimes for several years.

Gills: Fish need oxygen, but most fish cannot breathe air. Instead, they swallow water and push it out through their gills. The gills take the oxygen the fish needs from the water.

FISH FACTS

- Some fish lay eggs and others give birth to live young. Baby fish are often eaten, even by their parents, so they need to be moved to a separate tank if they are to survive.

- Surprisingly, fish can drown! Fish need oxygen and if there's not enough oxygen in the water, they will die.

Pectoral fins: These help to keep a fish balanced as it swims.

BEST FISH FOR BEGINNERS

If this is your first fish pal, it's best to start with freshwater fish. A saltwater tank needs more attention, and freshwater fish are **hardy** creatures. They will **adapt** more easily than saltwater fish if conditions in the tank aren't perfect.

Bloodfin tetras are peaceful fish that like to swim in schools of at least six. They enjoy a tank with plenty of plants for shelter and they mix well with other fish. They can jump, so you will need a tank with a tight-fitting cover.

White cloud mountain minnows prefer to swim in **schools** of eight or more. They like cold water and are easy to keep and **breed**. The males are usually smaller and more colorful than the females.

Zebra danios are fast, hardy fish that can survive in a wide range of conditions. They have even been sent into space! They **mate** for life and are easy to breed. They should be kept in groups of at least six.

Paradise gouramis are a colorful alternative to goldfish. Males often fight, so a male and two females are a good mix. They may attack other fish, so they are best kept alone or with fast fish that can easily escape them.

Red shiners are active fish that need a long and wide tank to swim in. They should be kept in groups of at least five. They are fin nippers, which means they like to nibble on the fins of other fish, so their tank mates need to be speedy swimmers!

Cherry barbs are peaceful little fish that like tanks with plenty of hiding places. They should be kept in schools of six to ten. Barbs are also fin nippers, so it's best not to keep them with long-finned fish.

Guppies are colorful fish that dart about and are easy to keep. They should live in groups of at least three and, unless you want lots of babies, you should make sure they are all the same sex.

Common goldfish are popular pets, but they belong in ponds because they can grow up to 16 inches (40 cm) long and live for more than 25 years! Fancy goldfish are smaller, but they still need big tanks and frequent water changes because they produce a lot of waste. Fancy goldfish are also slow swimmers, so they shouldn't be kept with other goldfish as they may not get enough food. As goldfish produce a lot of **ammonia**, they don't mix well with other tank mates either.

Siamese fighting fish are also known as bettas. They are brilliantly colored and the male fish have long, flowing fins. They breathe air from the surface and require warm water.

Swordtails are named after the male's sword-like tail. The best combination is a male and two or more females. They produce live young, but many babies get eaten, often by their own parents.

CHOOSING A HOME FOR YOUR FISH

You'll need to get your tank set up several weeks before bringing your fish home, but it's important to decide what type of fish you'd like first so you buy the right equipment to suit their needs.

WARM or COLD?

A coldwater tank is easier to set up as you won't need a heater if it's kept in a warm room. Be sure that it's away from sources of heat such as radiators or sunlight so the temperature stays stable. Warmwater tanks allow you to keep a greater range of fish, and many fish are happier and grow better in warmer water, even though they can survive at lower temperatures.

PET CHECK ☑

What you'll need:

- a tank with a well-fitting cover (tetras, barbs, and swordtails can jump)
- a light, so you can enjoy your fish at their colorful best
- an air pump to keep enough oxygen in the water
- a filter system
- gravel or sand
- decor (ornaments and hiding places)
- plants
- a thermometer
- a water-testing kit
- a net
- tank-cleaning equipment
- a bucket specifically for use with your fish tank
- a heater (if you've decided on a warmwater tank)

TANK SIZE

Check the charts on pages 14 and 15 to see how large your fish will grow and then figure out the size of aquarium you'll need. The usual rule is 1 inch (2.5 cm) of fish to 1 gallon (3.79 liters) of water, so you could have five guppies in a 10-gallon (37.9-liter) tank. Some fish like to live in schools, so you'll need space for a group of six or more.

POSITIONING THE TANK

Fish are sensitive to noise, so put the tank somewhere quiet. If you don't have a tank heater, keep your fish in a warm room where the temperature doesn't fall too low at night. A tank full of water is heavy, so it needs strong and stable support, close to an electrical outlet.

PET TALK

Please don't keep me in a bowl. The water surface is too small so there's not enough oxygen in the water—and you can't fit in a filter or a heater.

FURNISHING YOUR TANK

Tank decorations and plants don't just make an aquarium more fun for your fish. They also keep the water healthy by providing a home for friendly **bacteria**.

SUBSTRATE

A 2-inch (5 cm) layer of substrate, or sand or gravel on the bottom of the tank, creates a natural environment for your underwater pals and helps friendly bacteria grow. Food **particles** don't usually sink into sand and are removed by the filtering system, but gravel needs regular vacuuming to remove them.

PLANTS

Live plants remove harmful chemicals from the water, provide shelter for fish, and they also look nice! You can buy special substrate that contains food for plants. Don't wash the whitish slime off your plants because it is good bacteria that fish will sometimes eat. Just like fish, plants have their own special requirements, so learn what they need before you buy them.

PET TALK

Please don't put too much in my tank or I won't have enough space to swim around!

DECOR

You'll have to wait until your tank is ready before you collect your finny friends, but you can still have fun decorating their new home. Ornaments provide hidey-holes and shelter for shy fish, and they are places for good bacteria to grow.

LIGHTING

Live plants need light to survive, but too much increases the **algae** in a tank. Start with 12 hours a day of light and adjust this according to the algae growth. If your tank is in a sunny room, you'll only need to switch the light on when it gets darker. LED lights are best because they're cheap to run and don't raise the tank's temperature.

GETTING READY FOR YOUR FISH

Fish waste, old food, and rotting plants all add ammonia to tank water. Ammonia can kill fish, so you need to grow a helpful **colony** of bacteria to get rid of it. This is called **cycling** and it takes patience!

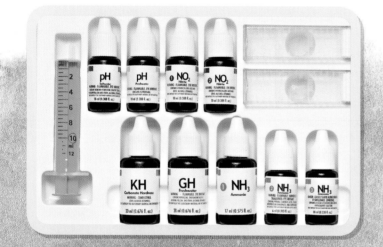

A BIT OF CHEMISTRY

Bacteria called Nitrosomonas change ammonia into chemicals called nitrites. Nitrites are also harmful to fish, so you need other bacteria, called Nitrobacter, to turn nitrites into chemicals called nitrates. You will need a water-testing kit to keep track of these levels. The level of nitrates in your tank should be below 20. See page 13 for more information on water testing.

GIVE YOUR BACTERIA A HOME

The friendly bacteria that keep your fish alive live in the substrate, on the tank walls, on ornaments, and in the filter. Put everything except the fish into the tank at the start of the cycling process.

FILL UP THE TANK

Tap water is best for fish tanks, but you'll need a **chlorine** remover. Chlorine kills bacteria, including the friendly ones you are trying to encourage! With an adult's assistance, fill your tank with the dechlorinated water and add 2 to 3 teaspoons (10 to 15 ml) of household ammonia. Wait for one hour and then test the ammonia levels in the water.

TEST, TEST, AND TEST AGAIN

After one week, you should see the ammonia levels going down and the nitrites going up. When the ammonia reaches zero, add 1 teaspoon (5 ml) of ammonia each day to feed your bacteria. Nitrites should rise, then fall, during the third or fourth week. Then start testing for nitrates. When the nitrates are climbing and the ammonia and nitrites are zero, you should change 60 to 80 percent of the water to bring the nitrate level to below 20. Leave the tank overnight, then add your fish.

TAKE CARE!

Ammonia is a very dangerous chemical, so an adult should help you when adding it to the tank. Instead of using ammonia, you can drop some fish flakes into the tank each day until you reach the proper ammonia reading.

SPEEDING THINGS UP

Cycling takes up to six weeks! You can speed it up if you have a friend with a healthy tank who can give you some substrate or ornaments already colonized by bacteria, but there's a risk of introducing snails and **parasites** to your tank. Living plants, such as Vallisneria and Hygrophila, are helpful because they absorb ammonia.

STOCKING YOUR AQUARIUM

Once you decide on a coldwater or warmwater tank, it's time to choose your fish. If you want to have different species of fish, you'll need to learn which ones can live together happily.

FINNY FRIENDS

Tanks of mixed fish are fun, but make sure they're all happy at the same temperature and won't attack one another. Fin nippers should never be kept with long-finned fish, and aggressive fish, such as paradise gouramis and Siamese fighting fish, should live with speedy swimmers that can dart for cover. All fish get stressed in overcrowded aquariums, so don't overstock your tank!

FISH FOR A COLDWATER TANK

Make sure the temperature in your tank doesn't drop too low at night. Bloodfin tetras, zebra danios, and cory catfish need a water temperature of at least 64°F (18°C).

Fish	Maximum length	Water temperature	Best tank mates
Bloodfin tetra	2 inches (5 cm)	64 to 75°F (18 to 24°C)	Peppered cory catfish
White cloud mountain minnow	1.5 inches (3.8 cm)	60 to 73°F (15.5 to 23°C)	Peppered cory catfish, zebra danio
Paradise gourami	4 inches (10 cm)	60 to 75°F (15.5 to 24°C)	Zebra danio if there's plenty of space
Zebra danio	2 inches (5 cm)	64 to 74°F (18 to 23.5°C)	White cloud mountain minnow
Red shiner	4 inches (10 cm)	59 to 77°F (15 to 25°C)	Zebra danio, white cloud mountain minnow
Peppered cory catfish (see page 16)	3 inches (7.5 cm)	64 to 77°F (18 to 25°C)	White cloud mountain minnow, bloodfin tetra

HEALTH CHECK

- Fish should be alert and active, and swim in a normal way.

- Avoid any fish that have cloudy or bulging eyes.

- Fish should not have any sores, spots, or ragged fins.

FISH FOR A HEATED TANK

Some fish that can survive in colder water also do well in a heated tank. Check that the maximum temperature these fish can cope with matches that of your warmwater tank.

Add fish to your tank a few at a time, starting with the hardiest, and keep testing the water.

Fish	Maximum length	Water temperature	Best tank mates
Cherry barb	2 inches (5 cm)	73 to 81°F (23 to 27°C)	White cloud mountain minnow, some tetras
Guppy	2 inches (5 cm)	64 to 82°F (18 to 28°C)	White cloud mountain minnow, some tetras, kuhli loach
Swordtail	5 inches (12.5 cm)	72 to 82°F (22 to 28°C)	Peppered cory catfish, guppy, some tetras
Siamese fighting fish	3 inches (7.5 cm)	75 to 86°F (24 to 30°C)	Peppered cory catfish
Kuhli loach (see page 16)	4 inches (10 cm)	77 to 82°F (25 to 28°C)	Most fish that are not large enough to eat them

THE CLEANUP CREW

Algae and snails are common problems in tanks, but there's an army of cleaners that will keep them under control. Most fish live in the middle and at the top of the water, so there's room at the bottom for these interesting creatures.

BOTTOM-DWELLERS

Cory catfish, such as the peppered cory, help keep tanks clean by eating algae and bits of leftover food. These peaceful bottom-feeders should be kept in groups of at least four, and need a sandy substrate so they don't damage their **barbels**.

Eel-like kuhli loaches are **nocturnal**. They search for dropped food at the bottom of the tank and in crevices, so filters and pumps should be covered with mesh so they can't get inside. They need a fine sand substrate because they love to dig holes and hide during the day.

HELPFUL SNAILS

The zebra nerite snail has a beautiful, striped shell and a big appetite for algae. Unlike other algae-eating snails, it won't attack your plants, but you may need to feed it algae wafers from time to time. The assassin snail (see page 21) will help you get rid of snail pests. If it runs out of snails to prey on, you'll need to feed it meaty foods.

SCAVENGER SHRIMP

Red cherry shrimp are scavengers that feed on algae and plant debris, while ghost shrimp clear up any leftover food. They both make peaceful tank mates for fish that are too small to eat them.

ADDING NEW TANK MATES

Rearrange the ornaments in your tank and feed your fish before you introduce newcomers, or **territorial** fish may attack them. Put the plastic bag holding your new pets into the aquarium and leave it unopened for 10 minutes, so they get used to the temperature.

Open the bag and pour in a cup of tank water, then reseal it and let it float for another 10 minutes. Keep repeating until the bag is full, then use a net to transfer the new tank mates to the aquarium. Don't mix any water from the bag into your tank water to avoid spreading snails or diseases.

FEEDING YOUR FISH

Like all animals, fish need the right food to stay healthy. Some only eat other creatures, while some will eat anything!

DON'T OVERFEED YOUR FISH

In the wild, fish may go for days without finding food, eating whenever they get the chance. Fish that overeat can suffer health problems, so giving them a small amount of food once or twice a day should be enough. Any leftover food can block your filter or rot in the tank. If any food is left after 10 minutes, scoop it up with a net and give your fish a bit less next time.

FEEDING NOCTURNAL FISH AND FRY

Fish that are active at night, such as kuhli loaches and some catfish, should be fed just before you turn the lights off. Fry, or baby fish, need special food because normal fish food is too large for them to eat.

CATFISH

GOLDFISH

SPECIALIST DIETS

Check what your new pets eat before bringing them home, and do some research to make sure you'll provide the best diet. Floating fish flakes are good for most fish that live at the top and in the middle of the tank, but bottom-feeders need food that sinks, and algae-eaters need algae wafers.

EATING EACH OTHER

A lot of fish eat smaller fish in the wild, so do some research to make sure that your pets don't end up as expensive food for their tank mates. None of your fish should be shorter than half the length of the largest. Aggressive fish, such as angelfish and cichlids, may take bites out of other fish, especially if they have long fins! Even small fish can be fin nippers.

KEEPING YOUR TANK CLEAN

Good tank maintenance will keep your pets healthy. If there's a buildup of algae, or if food and waste are floating in the water, it's time to take action.

CLEANING THE TANK

Only special tank-cleaning equipment should be used, as traces of soap or cleaning products could harm your fish. Get everything ready in advance and prepare the replacement water the day before so it's at the right temperature (see page 21). Here's what you'll need:

PET CHECK ☑

- algae scrubber and scraper
- gravel vacuum cleaner
- bucket
- replacement water

CLEAN YOUR TANK IN THIS ORDER:

- Unplug all electrical items.
- Remove 20 percent of the tank's water (see page 21).
- Remove ornaments, but leave live plants in the tank.
- Clean the inside of the glass with an algae scrubber and scraper.
- Twist the gravel vacuum through the gravel. The gravel will drop back into the tank while any debris goes into the bucket with the water. If you have sand instead of gravel, hold the vacuum hose above the surface of the sand so it only sucks up waste but not sand.
- Rub algae off the ornaments, then rinse the filter pad and ornaments in the water you removed from the aquarium.
- Replace the filter pad and ornaments.
- Plug everything back in, but leave the tank dark for a while. Tank cleaning is stressful for your underwater friends and the darkness will keep them calm.

WATER CHANGES

Aim to change about 20 percent of your tank's water every week. Never change it all because you will lose the friendly bacteria that keep your fish healthy. Never use water straight from the tap to replace it. Fill a container with water the day before so the chlorine can **evaporate**. You can also use a chlorine remover (see page 13). When the water is room temperature, it is ready for use in your tank.

PESKY SNAILS

Snails or their eggs can be unintentionally transferred to a tank when new fish or plants are added. Most snails don't need a mate to breed, so a single snail can soon become many snails! You can control them by hanging a lettuce leaf on the side of the glass overnight and removing any snails that are attached to it in the morning, or by using a snail trap. Fish such as Siamese fighting fish, and some loaches and catfish, eat snails. Or you could get an assassin snail to do the job!

Assassin snails

LOOKING AFTER YOUR FISH

Fish are not demanding pets but they rely on you to keep them healthy. The best way to avoid problems is to keep the tank clean and **quarantine** new fish before adding them to your aquarium.

FIN ROT

If a fish has ragged fins it may be suffering from fin rot. This infection is often caused by conditions in the tank such as bad water quality or overcrowding. Make sure none of the fish are nipping others, thoroughly clean the tank, and do a 30 percent water change. Buy a fin rot treatment and follow the instructions on the bottle. Keep testing the water quality and clean the tank regularly.

HOSPITAL TANK

Disease spreads quickly in an aquarium, so it's a good idea to keep a small tank as a hospital for sick fish. You'll need a cover, a heater, and a filter, and it's best to keep the filter in the main tank so it's already colonized with good bacteria. A small tank is useful for quarantining new fish before introducing them to the main tank, and for raising fry if your fish breed.

Freshwater fish parasite under microscope

WHITE SPOT DISEASE (ICH) AND VELVET

Ich and velvet are both diseases caused by parasites on a fish's skin. Fish in poor conditions or with a bad diet are most at risk. Take a close look if your fish start scratching themselves on rocks or ornaments. Fish with ich have small white spots that look like sand, and those with velvet have gold- or rust-colored film on their skin. You can buy treatments to kill the parasites.

ELECTRICAL SAFETY

Water and electricity are never a good mix, so follow these rules to make sure you stay safe! Ask an adult to make sure your tank is positioned correctly and safely. Always turn the power off when you're cleaning or maintaining the tank. Cables should have a "drip loop," so they loop down toward the floor and then back up to the electrical outlet. If any water drips from the tank, it will travel down the cable and drip onto the floor instead of into the outlet.

UNDERSTANDING YOUR FISH

Watching how your fish behave will give you a good idea of how they're feeling. In many cases, unusual behavior is caused by overcrowding, poor water quality, or the wrong tank mates.

SIAMESE FIGHTING FISH

HANGING AROUND AT THE SURFACE

If fish are hungry, or expect food at the same time each day, they might swim up to the surface when someone approaches. However, they may also swim to the surface if the water temperature is too cold lower down in the tank, so check the thermometer.

GULPING AIR

Labyrinth fish, including Siamese fighting fish and gouramis, breathe air from the surface because the water in their natural environment is low in oxygen. If other fish seem to be gasping for air, check if the tank is dirty or if the filter or air pump need fixing.

PEARL GOURAMI

BULLYING BEHAVIOR

If your fish are hiding, chasing others, or being chased, they may be stressed. Test the water for ammonia and check that it has enough oxygen. Some fish are naturally aggressive, so make sure they have suitable tank mates. If a male fish chases a female, he may want to mate with her or, if they have babies, he could become territorial to protect them. If a bottom-feeder doesn't get enough food, it may try to eat the slime coating that protects the skin of its tank mates.

LONERS AND SHOALERS

Some fish live in **shoals** or schools. This protects them from predators, and they won't be happy unless they're in a group of a certain size. This varies according to species, so check how many you will need. Male fish such as Siamese fighting fish and gouramis will fight rival males and may attack other fish, so should be kept alone or with one or two females.

25

DIY DECOR

You can buy all sorts of ornaments for your tank in a pet store, but why not use your imagination to make some of your own?

DECORATING DOS AND DON'TS

Fish are sensitive to chemicals, so any materials in your tank must be aquarium-safe. Avoid metal objects and anything that has been painted but not sealed. Rocks and driftwood may also affect the water so it's best to avoid them! Make sure there are no sharp edges that may scratch your fish, as injuries can lead to fin rot.

CREATE A COLORFUL BACKGROUND

Adding a background looks great and also helps fish that get scared if they see their reflection in the glass. Print out an image or draw your own to tape to the outside of your tank. Laminate your background to stop it from getting wet!

BRICK BUILDS

Use your imagination to create an underwater world with plastic bricks. You could build a shipwreck, a lost city, or a castle for your fish! To make sure the bricks are clean, soak them in a weak solution of bleach, rinse, and then leave them to dry. They should no longer smell of bleach.

HOMEMADE HIDEY-HOLES

Fish love places for hiding! You can make a cave by laying a new terra-cotta plant pot or a coffee mug on its side. Or try carving a door in half a coconut shell, making sure that all edges are smooth. Coconut shells need to be boiled in water for 20 minutes, drained, and reboiled three or four times until the water is clear.

FISH QUIZ

By now you should know lots of things about fish.

Test your knowledge by answering these questions:

1 **Where is a fish's caudal fin?**

a.   Under its body

b.   On its tail

c.   On its back

2 **Which of these may nip the fins of long-finned tank mates?**

a.   Red shiners

b.   White cloud mountain minnows

c.   Cory catfish

3 **Why shouldn't you keep fish in a bowl?**

a.   They get dizzy swimming in circles

b.   The surface is too small to provide enough oxygen in the water

c.   They bump into the sides

4 **Which of these chemicals is dangerous for fish?**

a.   Ammonia

b.   Nitrites

c.   Both of these

5 **Why don't zebra danios and kuhli loaches make good tank mates?**

a.   They don't like the same water temperature

b.   The danios will eat the kuhli loaches

c.   They will fight

6 Small white spots are a sign of which fishy disease?

a. Fin rot
b. Velvet
c. Ich

10 Why might fish be hanging around at the top of the tank?

a. The water is too dirty
b. The water is too cold lower down in the tank
c. There is too much algae in the tank

7 Why is the zebra nerite snail a useful tank mate?

a. It eats other snails
b. It eats algae
c. It eats leftover food

8 Why aren't fish flakes the best food for catfish?

a. They float and catfish are bottom-feeders
b. They don't like the taste
c. They only eat meat

9 What should you do when you introduce new fish to the tank?

a. Take all the other fish out of the tank first
b. Empty the bag of water containing the new fish straight into the tank
c. Rearrange the ornaments in the tank

QUIZ ANSWERS

1 Where is a fish's caudal fin?

b. On its tail

2 Which of these may nip the fins of long-finned tank mates?

a. Red shiners

3 Why shouldn't you keep fish in a bowl?

b. The surface is too small to provide enough oxygen in the water

4 Which of these chemicals is dangerous for fish?

c. Both of these

5 Why don't zebra danios and kuhli loaches make good tank mates?

a. They don't like the same water temperature

6 Small white spots are a sign of which fishy disease?

c. Ich

7 Why is the zebra nerite snail a useful tank mate?

b. It eats algae

8 Why aren't fish flakes the best food for catfish?

a. They float and catfish are bottom-feeders

9 What should you do when you introduce new fish to the tank?

c. Rearrange the ornaments in the tank

10 Why might fish be hanging around at the top of the tank?

b. The water is too cold lower down in the tank

LEARNING MORE

BOOKS

MacAulay, Kelley and Bobbie Kalman. *Goldfish*. Crabtree Publishing, 2005.

Rau, Dana Meachen and Joanna Ponto. *Kids Top 10 Pet Fish (American Humane Association Top 10 Pets for Kids)*. Enslow Elementary, 2015.

Titmus, Dawn. *Fish (Cool Pets for Kids)*. PowerKids Press, 2018.

WEBSITES

https://kids.nationalgeographic.com/animals/hubs/fish
This site offers games, images, videos, and tons of information about fish.

www.vetbabble.com/small-pets/fish/goldfish-care-guide
This site is full of helpful information about goldfish care.

GLOSSARY

adapt To become used to new conditions

algae A type of plant that grows in aquariums

ammonia A chemical that is produced in a fish tank when food, algae, and fish poop break down

bacteria Microscopic living things

barbel A whisker-like organ on some fish

breed To make babies

chlorine A chemical in tap water that kills bacteria

colony A group of bacteria that grows together

cycling Growing a colony of friendly bacteria

evaporate When liquid turns to vapor

hardy Able to survive in difficult conditions

mate When living things partner in order to breed

nocturnal An animal that sleeps during the day and is active at night

parasite An animal that lives in or on another creature and feeds from it

particles Tiny bits of matter that make up everything in the universe

predator An animal that hunts other creatures

prey An animal that is hunted by other animals

quarantine Separating an animal from others to stop illness or disease from spreading

school A group of fish that swim closely together, with all fish following the same path

shoal A group of fish that swim in the same direction, but individual fish may change direction

species A group of closely related organisms

stable Describes something that is firm and secure

territorial The behavior of an animal that is defending its territory

vertebrate An animal with a spine

INDEX